Upaniṣad Series

ĪŚĀVĀSYOPANIṢAD

Including the original verses, construed text (anvaya) with a literal word by word translation, transliteration, English rendering of each stanza, copious notes, Introduction and Appendix

BY

SWĀMĪ ŚARVĀNANDA

SRI RAMAKRISHNA MATH

16, RAMAKRISHNA MATH ROAD,

MADRAS-600 004. : : INDIA

Published by
The President
Sri Ramakrishna Math
Mylapore, Chennai-4

XVI-2M 3C-5-2002
ISBN 81-7120-499-6

Printed in India at
Sri Ramakrishna Math Printing Press
Mylapore, Chennai-4

PREFACE TO THE FIRST EDITION

ORIGINALLY this series of Upaniṣads appeared in the pages of the *Vedānta Kesari*, the organ of the Ramakrishna Math, Madras, and subsequently these Upaniṣads were reprinted in book form with some additions and alterations. It has been acknowledged by all scholars that the Upaniṣads constitute the supreme achievement of Hindu thought. The sublimity of their soaring meditation, the infinite range of their outlook on life, their fearless exposition of Soul-consciousness, their determined assertion of the verities of Existence and lastly their broad synthesis of knowledge and experience, have all joined to evoke towards them in the Hindu heart a feeling of profound awe and respect, and made it love them as Divine Revelations from the immemorial past. Moreover, to an aspirant of spiritual truth, the Upaniṣads shed a light unseen in any other scripture or literature of the world. It has, therefore, been felt as the supreme need of these times to popularise the Upaniṣadic lore. With this object in view, we have been publishing the original texts of the principal Upaniṣads with suitable annotations in the *Vedānta Keśari*. Some of these have been brought out in book form, and others also will follow.

The Upaniṣads, as the name implies, embody esoteric spiritual knowledge meant for reflection and contemplation, and hence the deeper a man dives into the significance of the passages of these scriptures in meditation, the greater the hidden meanings he finds in them. And so the sole object of the editor of this series in annotating the Upaniṣads is more to help such persons as are desirous of plunging into their spiritual contents than to satisfy the superficial reader or the mere scholar.

ŚARVĀNANDA

INTRODUCTION

WHAT are the Vedas, of which the Upaniṣads constitute the end and aim, the very Crest-jewel? What is their source? What are their features? The great Sāyaṇācārya, to whose elucidation the present understanding of their meaning is mainly due, defines the Veda as that literature which sheds light on the transcendental means of achieving what is wished for and avoiding what is disliked.[1] The role of the Revealed Scripture lies beyond the spheres of perception and inference, for it illumines us about 'all the divinities, moral and spiritual duties of man, and Absolute Truth.'[2] Since man is imperfect, human deliverances, however exalted they may be, can hardly be accepted as final and infallible. Therefore on questions regarding transcendental facts a self-manifest, inherently valid, eternally existing, divinely inspired Veda alone can be

---

1. इष्टप्राप्त्यनिष्टपरिहारयो: अलौकिकं उपायं यो ग्रन्थो वेदयति स वेद: । अलौकिकपदेन प्रत्यक्षानुमाने व्यावर्त्येते ।

Sāyaṇa's Taittirīyasaṁhitā bhāṣya, p. 2

अलौकिकपुरुषार्थोपायं वेत्त्यनेनेति वेदशब्दानर्वचनम् ।
प्रत्यक्षेणानुमित्या वा यस्तूपायो न बुध्यते ।
एनं विदन्ति वेदेन तस्माद् वेदस्य वेदता ।

Sāyaṇa's Ṛg-Bhāṣya, Introduction.

2. सकलदेवतानां धर्मस्य परब्रह्मतत्वस्य च प्रतिपादकं वेदम् ।

Ibid

considered infallible and conclusively authoritative.[1] The continuous unfoldment of the predominantly religious and spiritual culture of India for millenniums, governing the thought and conduct of the race, working through the moral and religious impulses of the entire people and drawing them ever to the realization of the highest values of life, attests to the greatness and penetrative influence of the Vedas.

The Vedas are transmitted from beginningless antiquity through a continuous chain of teachers and pupils, who, relying upon the statements in the Vedas themselves, considered them to be eternal and *apauruṣeya*, i.e., having no human source. Of those who hold fast to this theory of eternality, some substantiate their position by arguing that since the Vedas are the only source of our knowledge of Dharma and Brahman which are eternal, and since the relation between Word and its meaning is also eternal, the Vedas are eternal in language and content. There are others who view the unworldly and spiritual principles enunciated in them to be eternal and timeless, they do not subscribe to the other part of the argument, viz., the eternality of the language of the Veda, which, they would assert, is but the composition (vākya) of *ṛṣis* or āptapuruṣas—reliable and selfless personages who have realized those truths for themselves.

---

1. ब्रह्मणो निर्दोषत्वेन वेदस्य कर्तृदोषासम्भवात् स्वतः सिद्धं प्रामाण्यं तदवस्थम्—

Sāyaṇa's Aitareya-brāhmaṇa bhāṣya, p. 2.

According to the famous Puruṣa-sūkta, Ṛk, Yajus and Sāman were generated at the beginning of creation from a mental sacrifice of adoration performed by the divine Prajāpatis and sages with the Supreme Being as the material of the offering. The Śvetāśvataropaniṣad[1] states that the Supreme Being creates Bahmā and communicates to him the Vedas. The Bṛhadāraṇyaka IV. v. 11 has: "As from a fire kindled......smoke issues, even so, the Ṛgveda etc..... are all the breath of this infinite Reality." The Brahma-sūtra I. 1. 3 declares that Brahman is the source of the Vedas; and I. 3. 29 of the same book affirms them to be eternal. The Mimāmsā-sūtra I. 1. 18 establishes the eternality of the Word. The first stanza of Srimad-bhāgavata, voicing the view of the Purāṇas in general, states that God, the Supreme Truth, caused the Vedas to appear in the mind of Brahmā, the first 'poet.' Smṛtis generally state that the eternally existing Vedas were remembered by the Creator at the beginning of the cycle of creation and were transmitted to the world through a chain of successors of teachers and learners. Śrī Śaṅkara in his introduction to the Gītā-bhāṣya, speaks of the imparting of the Religion of Works and the Religion of Renunciation, constituting the contents of the Vedas, to Prajāpatis like Marīci and to sages like Sanaka, by the Lord Nārāyaṇa, immediately after the creation of the universe, and also of the subsequent dissemination of the Vedic lore through that channel. These various accounts given in the authoritative books of the past speak for the

1. vi. 18.

inspirational quality of the Vedas and the great veneration with which they were looked upon from the dawn of the Hindu civilization.

Even though the orthodox teachers of India do not assent to the dialectic differences and chronological strata recognised by Western scholars in the body of the Vedas they have their own logical appellations, divisions and classifications of the various parts of the Vedic literature. The Veda is generally spoken of as vidyā (from the root 'vid' meaning to know, reflect, possess, be) denoting wisdom that is gained by intuition or instruction. When taken as a vidyā, the Veda has two phases, a higher one and a lower one, parā-and aparā, the one connoting divine wisdom and the other knowledge of everything else that tends to it. Śāstra is from the root 'śās', meaning to wish, command or teach; and hence the Veda as a Śāstra is either ajñāta-jñāpaka or apravṛtta-pravartaka, that is revelational or mandatory. The Vedas are also known commonly as Nigama, Śruti and Āmnāya. Nigama implies a settled text handed down from beginningless antiquity. Śruti denotes a revealed text heard by the pupil from the teacher. Āmnāya is what is learned by repetition and reflection. Almost synonymous with aparā- and parā Vidyā is the division into karma-kāṇḍa and jñāna-kāṇḍa, work-section and knowledge-section, the former dealing with religious rites and duties and the latter with God, Soul and Nature. It is generally held that this twofold division coincides with the external division into non-Upaniṣadic and Upaniṣadic Vedic literature. Such a view cannot be taken as well-marked and precise, since there is ritualistic material interspersed in certain portions of some of the Upaniṣads and esoteric and philosophic ideals in the Saṁhitās. So Muktikopaniṣad recognizes that "like oil in the sesamum seed Vedānta is established essentially in every part of the Veda"[1]. We are therefore to take these names and divisions more as dominated by the spirit and purposes that govern them rather than as mere formal or structural matter.

This leads us to the customary classification based upon the form, purport and style of the Vedic literature. These are the four well-known divisions of the Veda into Ṛk, Yajus, Sāman and Atharva: Mantra or Samhitā, Brāhmaṇa, Āraṇyaka and Upaniṣad; and caraṇa'śākhā or bheda. Of the first division, the words 'Ṛk' means a laudatory verse, Yajus, a liturgical passage or formula (mostly prose and sometimes metrical) and Sāman, a melody. These three species of compositions in their collective form were also called in a secondary sense Ṛk-Yajus-and-Sāma-Saṁhitās. Finally by extension the Brāhmaṇas annexed to these Ṛk-Yajus-Sāma and Atharva -samhitās, the Āraṇyakas supplementary to them, and the Upaniṣads, either embedded in, terminated by, or affiliated to each of them, were also included by the name of the respective Veda to which they belonged.

The self-manifest Veda, which according to the purāṇic account, was a unified plenary revelation made to

---

1. तिलेषु तैलवत् वेदे वेदान्तः सुप्रतिष्ठितः I. 9.

Brahmā in the beginning, suffered much obscurity in subsequent ages, due to the confusion and want of care on the part of the learners. At the commencement of the Dvāparayuga, therefore, the great sage Kṛṣṇa-dvaipāyana (Vyāsa) resuscitated it by clarifying and facilitating its study by his methodical arrangement in the four divisions, Ṛk, Yajus, Sāman and Atharva, and by making his four disciples Paila, Vaiśampāyana, Jaimini and Sumantu the recipients and transmitters of the four Vedas in the respective order. Disciples of these lineal heads, in course of time, multiplied and formed into groups, separating from each other and giving rise to various śākhās or branches. Each of these śākhās had its own reduction or collection of the given Veda preserved as its heirloom, differing not a little from the other. These were named according to the śākhā (school) to which it belonged, as Kaṭha, Kauthuma, Vājasaneya, Mādhyandina and the like. The Muktikopaniṣad (verses 12 & 13) records as there having existed twenty-one such śākhās for the Ṛg-veda, ninety-four for Black Yajur-veda, fifteen for White Yajur-veda, one thousand for Sāma-veda and fifty for Atharva-veda; about most of these we know nothing at present except this bare mention.

The next division, partly based on style and parly on purport, is the one into Mantra and Brāhmaṇā[1]. The

1. मन्त्रश्च ब्राह्मणं चेति द्वौ भागौ—तेन मन्त्रतः।
अन्यत् ब्राह्मणम्, इत्येतद् भवेत् ब्राह्मणलक्षणम्।
Aitareya-brāhmaṇa-bhāṣya.

Kalpa-śāstra defines the Veda as constituting of Mantra and Brāhmaṇa. This division is internal to the above said fourfold division; for, each Veda has its Mantra and Brāhmaṇa portions, the former comprising all chants and invocations (i.e. Mantras) and the latter everything else with the exception of the Mantras. The first three Saṁhitās—by which we are to understand the three canonical texts designated as Ṛk, Yajus and Sāman, collections embodying the invocatory stanzas and the ritualistic formulas sung or uttered, arranged in hymns, books and other literary divisions—had even a functional basis. The popular viniyoga or use of the Veda was for the meticulous performance of painstaking and complicated sacrificial ceremonials which were believed to bring about directly or indirectly abhyudaya and niśreyasa, i.e., temporal prosperity and the highest good of life; and so all parts of the Veda had to be interpreted in such a way as they might find place in this scheme either as invocatory, eulogistic or directive in their application. The four Vedas thus came to be associated with the four priests who were indispensable to the performance of a sacrifice, yajña. They are Hotṛ, the reciter of the solemn hymns, Adhvaryu or the performer of the material part of the sacrifice with the help of liturgical formulas, Udgātṛ, the chanter of the Sāman songs and Brahman, who, although by name is associated with the Atharva-veda, is the superintendent of the entire sacrifice—"the very embodiment of the sacrificial art and Vedic lore in general so as to be able to advise the other priests and rectify any mistake committed during the performance."

Among the Saṁhitās or collection, Rg-veda is by far the most important; for a considerable portion of the other Vedas are either repeated or adapted from it. According to the current Śākala school, it has 1028 metrical hymns sung in praise of various devatās or aspects of the Divine. These hymns of varying length, the longest having 52 stanzas, are arranged into ten Maṇḍalas or Books of which the tenth is specially interesting for the philosophical and esoteric material contained therein, although such information is not entirely absent in other parts too. To the Ṛg-veda belong Aitareya, Kauṣītakī, Paiṅgi and Śāṅkhyāyana Brāhmaṇas. The Aitareya and *kauṣītakī* Āraṇyakas supplement the Brāhmaṇas of the same names. The Aitareya and Kauṣī-takī Upaniṣads are taken in as some of the concluding sections of theĀraṇyakas bearing those names.

The Taittirīya saṁhitā of the Yajur-veda, also called Kṛṣṇa-yajur-veda, is the book of the performing priest or Adhvaryu, and is, for the most part, in prose. Mainly sacrificial in purpose, it is a mixture of ritualistic formulas and explanations. There is another important book of the Yajur-veda called the Śukla-yajur-veda in forty chapters, with its contents systematically arranged in a liturgical order. The Kṛṣṇa-yajur-veda has the Taittirīya-Bhāllava-Śāṭyāyana-Maitrāyaṇa and Kaṭha-brāhmaṇas, of which the first is the most well-known, its contents being of such a nature as could well be considered supplementary to its cognate Saṁhitā.The Taittirīya-āraṇyaka is its appendage, in which is embedded the important Taittirīya-upaniṣad. There is also a Maitrāyaṇi-upaniṣad. The Śukla-yajur-veda, now chiefly preserved in the Mādhyandina and Kāṇva schools, has the famous Śatapatha-brāhmaṇa terminating in the monumental Bṛhadāraṇyaka which is an Āraṇyaka and an Upaniṣad of great importance.

The Sāma-veda-samhitā is taken directly (excepting the seventy-five original verses) from the eighth and ninth Maṇḍalas of the Ṛg-veda and set to the mode of Sāman chants designed to be sung by the Udgātṛ priest. Eight short Brāhmaṇas (Sāmavidhana, Mantra, Ārṣeya, Vamśa, Daivatādhyāya, Talavakāra, Tāṇḍya and Samhitopaniṣad) are known to belong to it, explaining chiefly the duties of the priest of that Veda and other allied materials. No Āraṇyaka is known now to belong to it; but the famous Chāndogyopaniṣad and Kenopaniṣad are very important supplements of the Sāma-veda. Unlike the other three Vedas, Atharva-veda has no important part to play in the yajña, and the brahman priest, associated with it, has to function more comprehensively, as has been mentioned above. According to the current Śaunaka-śākhā, Atharva-veda-samhitā has 760 hymns of 6000 stanzas distributed over 20 chapters; of this total number 1200 stanzas are repetitions from the Ṛk-samhitā and a sixth of the whole work is in prose. It chiefly deals with occult matters, but there are to be found beautiful philosophical verses also in the book. This Veda also has not got any Āraṇyaka—at least known to us at present. Three very well-known Upaniṣads, Muṇḍaka, Māṇḍūkya and Praśna are considered as belonging to it. However, there is one Gopathabrāhmaṇa related to it, the importance of which is not very high in comparison with that of others.

The Brāhmaṇas aim at the intepretation of the texts supplied by the samhitās; they are, therefore exegetical and commentative. They describe the minute details of sacrificial ceremonies explaining their origin and hidden meaning and illustrating their value and potency by citing itihāsas or past stories. Sāyaṇa quotes a definition of Brāhmaṇa,[1] which is not very conclusive as he himself admits. It is therefore safely asserted, "All that is not Mantra is Brāhmaṇa" Many of the Brāhmaṇas known at present (about 16) generally treat about more or less a common stock of material with variations in treatment and elaboration.

The Āraṇyakas occupy an intermediate position between the Brāhmaṇas and Upaniṣads in form and spirit. They too are ritualistic in content like the Brāhmaṇas, but the material part is suppressed. In these Forest Books, 'the symbolic and spiritual aspect of the sacrificial cults are meditated upon, and the meditation takes the place of the performance of the sacrifice'.[2] The Araṇyakas

---

1. हेतुर्निर्वचनं निन्दा प्रशंसा संशयो विधिः ।
परक्रिया पुराकल्पो व्यवधारणकल्पना ।

Sāyaṇa's Intro. to the Ṛg. Veda.

ब्राह्मणानि कल्पान् गाथा नाराशंसीरितिहासपुराणानीति ।

Āśvalāyana-gṛhya-sūtra, III, 3. This is taken to be the definition of Brāhmaṇa.

2. Radhakrishnan: Indian Philosophy, Vol. I, p. 65.

are to be recited by those who have taken the vow (*vrata*) of the recluse and therefore (due perhaps to their superior sanctity also) they are designed for the *vānaprasthins* living in the solitude of forests. In general they share the subject-matter and treatment of the Upaniṣads also. From the point of subject-matter a clear demarcation line cannot be drawn between the two.

The Upaniṣads are the sum and substance of all true wisdom. Of the ten most authoritative Upaniṣads now authentically known to have been explained by Śri Śaṅkarācārya, five are parts of some well-known Samhitā or Āraṇyaka. According to tradition,[1] Upaniṣads are 1180, one for each śākhā of the Vedas; but only about 200 are brought to light[2] till now, many of which clearly bear the stamp of modernity. Of these, 108 are deemed worthy of careful study. They are all commented on by one Upaniṣad-brahmendra. The Muktikopaniṣad associates each one of them with one Veda or other, though only five, as we have noted, are actually seen as part of the Veda in its existing form. But there is evidence to believe that some more might have been part of some Saṁhitā or Brāhmaṇa in the past and from which they were separated and became detached subsequently.

THE ĪŚĀVĀSYOPANIṢAD. This particular Upaniṣad derives its name from the opening word of its first

1. Muktikopaniṣad, verse 14
2. By the Theosophical Publishing House, Adyar.

Mantra. In all collections and enumerations of the Upaniṣads it occupies the first place, owing partly perhaps to the great spiritual significance of its contents and partly to the fact that it is the only Upaniṣad that is found as an integral part of a Saṁhitā,[1] which fact gives it the other name, Saṁhitopaniṣad. It is the last chapter of the Sukla-yajur-veda-Saṁhitā. The Upaniṣads that are in verses (the most important ones, of course) are called the Mantropaniṣads. Iśāvāsya is the Mantropaniṣad[2] *par excellence.*

According to Śaṅkaracarya's analysis (whose commentary we have mainly followed in our explanations), this Upaniṣad lays down two paths for spiritual aspirants —one for the jñānins *i.e.* those who are the exclusive adherents of the path of knowledge, and the other for those who have not attained the necessary internal development needed to renounce desires and adopt that exalted way. A jñānin of that type is identical with a Sannyāsin. He is absolved from the performance of all

1. There are however some differences by way of variant readings and others in the text as it appears in the Vājasaneyi-saṁhitā and in the Upaniṣads as commented on by Saṅkarācārya. Mantras 9, 10 and 11 of the Saṁhitā text appear as Mantras 12, 13 and 14 of the Upaniṣad and *vice-versa.* The second half of the fifteenth Mantra and all the lines of the sixteenth Mantra except the last one, are not in the Saṁhitā text. The last five verses, just as in the Upaniṣad, are found in the Bṛhadāraṇyakopaniṣad 5-15-1.

2. Srimadbhagavata, VIII, I. 9 & 17.

sacrificial rites. Repeated study of the Upaniṣadic texts and reflection and contemplation on the real nature of the Ātman are the only activities that engage his attention. And the first verse and the verses from the fourth to the eighth (both included), which describe the nature of the Ātman, are meant for him. The rest of the Upaniṣad has in view all other persons who are bound to the world by the desire to enjoy it. These men who are attracted by the things of the world, worship God as a person with the aim of securing through His grace worldly happiness and spiritual bliss in the form of final emancipation from the round of births and deaths. They, as it is laid down in the second verse, should perform sacrificial rites and duties and at the same time acquire knowledge (*Vidyā*) about the various divinities and the supreme Divinity. By pursuing this discipline they will attain the highest heaven of Brahmā after death, as it is spoken of in the last verse of the Upaniṣad.

Owing to the terseness and the obscurity of many of the concepts found in this Upaniṣad many of its stanzas are liable to be interpreted differently, if one does not accept the fundamental premise of Saṅkarācārya regarding the two paths—that of knowledge and that of work—and their mutual opposition. In the appendix at the end of the book, we have given another interpretation of the Upaniṣad, synthesising work and knowledge in the light of the types of spiritual perfection we come across, the passive type and the active type.

3

NOTE ON TRANSLITERATION

In this book Devanāgarī characters are transliterated according to the scheme adopted by the International Congress of Orientalists at Athens in 1919 and since then generally acknowledged to be the only rational and satisfactory one. In it the inconsistency, irregularity and redundancy of English spelling are ruled out: f, q, w, x and z are not called to use; one fixed value is given to each letter. Hence a, e, i and g always represent अ, ए, इ and ग् respectively and never ए, इ, ऐ and ज or other values which they have in English; t and d are always used for त् and द् only. One *tilde*, one accent, four macrons and ten dots (2 above, 8 below) are used to represent adequately and correctly all Sanskrit letters. The letter c alone represents च्. Since the natural function of h will be to make the aghoṣa ghoṣa (*e.g.*., kh, ch, ṭh, th, ph, gh, jh, ḍh, dh, bh), it would be an anomaly for a scientific scheme to use it in combinations like ch and sh for giving च् and ष values: hence ch here is छ् and s, h स्, ह. The vowel ऋ, is represented by ṛ because ri, legitimate for रि only, is out of place, and the singular ṛi is an altogether objectionable distortion. The *tilde* over n represents ञ्, ñ.

Accent mark over s gives श्, ś; dots above m and n give anusvāra, (—) ṁ and ङ्, ṅ, respectively. Dots below h and r give visarga (:) ḥ, and ऋ, ṛ, respectively. Dots below s, n, t and d give their corresponding cerebrals ष्, ण्, ट् and ड्, ṣ, ṇ, ṭ, and ḍ; and macrons over a, i, u and ṛ give ā, ī, ū, and ṝ respectively. Macrons are not used to lengthen the quantity of e and o because they always have the long quantity in Sanskrit. Sanskrit words are capitalized only where special distinctiveness is called for, as in the opening of a sentence, title of books, etc. The scheme of transliteration in full is as follows:

अ a, आ ā, इ i, ई ī, उ u, ऊ ū, ऋ ṛ, ॠ ṝ, ए e, ओ o, ऐ ai, औ au,—ṁ, : ḥ, क् k, ख् kh, ग् g, घ् gh, ङ् ṅ, च् c, छ् ch, ज् j, झ् jh; ञ् ñ, ट् ṭ, ठ् ṭh, ड् ḍ, ढ् ḍh, ण् ṇ, त् t, थ् th, द् d, ध् dh, न् n, प् p, फ् ph, ब् b, भ् bh, म् m, य् y, र् r, ल् l, व् v, श् ś, ष् ṣ, स् s, ह् h.

। ओं तत् सत् ।

Om tat Sat

Peace Invocation

ओं पूर्णमदः पूर्णमिदं पूर्णात् पूर्णमुदच्यते ।
पूर्णस्य पूर्णमादाय पूर्णमेवावशिष्यते ॥
ओं शान्तिः । शान्तिः । शान्तिः ॥

Oṁ pūrṇamadaḥ pūrṇamidaṁ
pūrṇāt pūrṇam udacyate
pūrṇasya pūrṇam ādāya
pūrṇam ev'āvaśiṣyate

Om śāntiḥ śāntiḥ śāntiḥ ॥

ओं *om* Om पूर्णम् *pūrṇam* infinite अदः *adaḥ* that पूर्णम् *pūrṇam* infinite इदम् *idam* this. पूर्णात् ***pūrṇāt*** From the infinite पूर्णम् *pūrṇam* the whole (universe) उदच्यते *udacyate* has come out, पूर्णस्य *pūrṇasya* Of the infinite पूर्णम् *pūrṇam* the whole (universe) आदाय *ādāya* having taken पूर्णम् *pūrṇam* the infinite एव *eva* alone अवशिष्यते *avaśiṣyate* remains. ओं *oṁ* Om शान्तिः *śāntiḥ* peace.

The invisible is the Infinite, the visible too is the Infinite. From the Infinite, the visible universe of infinite extension has come out. The Infinite remains the same, even though the infinite universe has come out of it.

Om! Peace! Peace! Peace!

ĪŚAVĀSYOPANIṢAD

ॐ ईशा वास्यमिदꣳ सर्वं यत्किञ्च जगत्यां जगत् ।
तेन त्यक्तेन भुञ्जीथा मा गृधः कस्यस्विद् धनम् ॥ १ ॥

Om Īśā vāsyaṁ idaṁ sarvaṁ yatkiñ ca jagatyām jagat ।
tena tyaktena bhuñjīthā mā gṛdhaḥ kasyasvid dhanam ॥ 1 ॥

जगत्याम् *jagatyām* In the world यत् किं च *yat kim ca* whatsoever जगत् *jagat* changeful (अस्ति *asti* is), इदं सर्वम् *idaṁ sarvam* all this ईशा *īśa* with the Lord वास्यम् *vāsyam* should be enveloped. तेन त्यक्तेन *tena tyaktena* By that renunciation भुञ्जीथा: *bhuñjīthāḥ* support (yourself), कस्यस्वित् *kasyasvit* of any one धनम् *dhanam* wealth मा *mā* do not गृधः *gṛdhaḥ* covet.

Whatever[1] there is changeful in this ephemeral world,—all that must be enveloped by the Lord. By this renunciation[2] (of the world), support[3] yourself. Do[4] not covet the wealth of anyone.[5]

[NOTES — This passage refers to the duty of the Sannyāsin who is competent to devote himself exclusively to the contemplation of the Ātman.

1. *Whatever there is etc.*—Just as the bad odour of a piece of sandal-wood, produced by continuous contact with water, is covered by its inherent fragrant smell on its being rubbed on a stone, so also the changeful and imperfect world of duality is to be obliterated by its being enveloped, through contemplation, by the Divinity that is inherent in it as well as in the self of the contemplator. The expression 'changeful' applied to the world suggests by contrast that the Lord is the one changeless substratum in the flux of Nature. The word 'envelopes' signifies that the Lord is both immanent and transcendent.

2. *Renunciation*—Contemplation of this kind presupposes the renunciation of worldly life and desires pertaining to it.

3. *Support yourself*—Renunciation helps one to realise the Ātman and attain the bliss born of it. Hence the Sannyāsin is asked to support himself by renunciation in contrast to worldly men who support themselves by the satisfaction of desires.

4. *Do not covet etc.*—The Sannyāsin is to seek bliss in renunciation, and not in wealth which is the source of all worldly satisfactions.

5. *Anyone*—Implies what may belong to oneself as well as to others.]

कुर्वन्नेवेह कर्माणि जिजीविषेच्छतꣳ समाः ।
एवं त्वयि नान्यथेतोऽस्ति न कर्म लिप्यते नरे ॥ २ ॥

Kurvann ev'eha karmāṇi jijīviṣec chataṁ samāḥ
evaṁ tvayi n'ānyath'eto'sti na karma lipyate nare ll 2 ll

इह *iha* In this world कर्माणि *karmāṇi* (scripture-ordained) works (such as agnihotra etc.) कुर्वन् *kurvan* performing एव *eva* alone शतम् *śatam* a hundred समाः *samāḥ* years जिजीविषेत् *jijīviṣet* should desire to live. एवम् *evam* thus त्वयि *tvayi* you नरे *nare* man (wishing to live a hundred years) इतः *itaḥ* than this (performance of religious rites) न *na* not अन्यथा *anyathā* other alternative अस्ति *asti* is (येन *yena* by which) कर्म *karma* work न *na* not लिप्यते *lipyate* stains.

Only performing scripture-ordained[1] works, should one desire to live a hundred[2] years. Thus, and in no other way, can you be free from the taint[3] of evil deeds, as long as you are fond[4] of your human life. 2

[NOTES—In contrast to the previous passage, this one, according to Saṅkara, refers to those who are incapable of complete renunciation and absorption in the Ātman and have, as a consequence, to be devoted to righteous works by which they can attain purity of mind, and thereby knowledge ultimately.

2. *Scripture-ordained works*—Strictly speaking they are the necessary and occasional rites like *agnihotra* (maintenance of sacred fire) and other duties ordained by the

scriptures for house-holders. From a different point of view we may, however, include all altruistic works too.

2. *Hundred years*—This is the full span of human life according to the Vedas. To desire to live a hundred years means to have worldly attachments. This is to be contrasted with the attitude of a true Sannyāsin who has neither like nor dislike for both life and death.

3. *Taint of evil deeds*—A man who is not capable of complete absorption in the Ātman can save himself from stagnation and positive evil deeds, only if he engages himself in meritorious or altruistic works.

4. *Fond of your human life*—In contrast to the Sannyāsin who has given up all clinging to life itself.

According to some, this passage refers to Karmayoga or the path of desireless action elaborated in the Bhagavad gītā.]

असुर्या नाम ते लोका अन्धेन तमसावृताः।
तांस्ते प्रेत्याभिगच्छन्ति ये के चात्महनो जनाः ॥ ३ ॥

Asuryā nāma te lokā andhena tamas'āvṛtāḥ
tāṁs te prety'ābhigacchanti ye ke c'ātmahano janāḥ ॥ 3 ॥

असुर्याः *asuryāḥ* Belonging to the Asuras (demoniac) अंधेन तमसा *andhena tamasā* with the blinding darkness आवृताः *āvṛtāḥ* shrouded नाम *nāma* verily ते *te* those लोकाः *lokāḥ* births (सन्ति *santi* are). ये के *ye ke* whoever च *ca* and जनाः *janāḥ* persons आत्महनः

ātmahanaḥ slayers of Ātman (सन्ति *santi* are) ते *te* they प्रेत्य *pretya* after death तान् *tān* those (worlds) अभिगच्छन्ति *abhigacchanti* attain.

Verily, those births are demoniac,[1] enshrouded[2] in blinding darkness. Those[3] who slay the Self attain to them after death. 3

[NOTES—This refers to the second type of persons viz., those who are qualified only for work.

1. *Demoniac*—The word in the original is *asuryāḥ* meaning, 'of the *Asuras* or demons.' *Asuras* are noted for their attachment to sensual enjoyment. The births in various spheres, high and low, are conducive only to the life of the senses. Hence they are called 'demoniac' in contrast to the absolute state of emancipation.

2. *Enshrouded in blinding darkness*—In contrast to illumination that follows the realisation of the Ātman.

3. *Those who slay the Self*—Every one who is indifferent to the realisation of the Ātman, his own essential nature, may be described as committing spiritual suicide.

The purport of the passage is that those who have not realised the Self and are therefore competent only for work, will be reborn in different spheres, and this is a condition infinitely inferior to the realisation of the Self.]

अनेजदेकं मनसो जवीयो
नैनद्देवा आप्नुवन् पूर्वमर्षत् ।
तद्धावतोऽन्यानत्येति तिष्ठत्
तस्मिन्नपो मातरिश्वा दधाति ॥ ४ ॥

Anejad ekaṁ manaso javīyo
n'ainad devā āpnuvan pūrvam arṣat
tad dhāvato'nyān atyeti tiṣṭhat
tasminn apo mātariśvā dadhāti ॥ 4 ॥

(तत् *tat* That Ātman) एकम् *ekam* one अनेजत् *anejat* motionless (immutable) मनसः *manasaḥ* than mind जवीयः *javīyaḥ* faster देवाः *devāḥ* the senses एनत् *enat* this न आप्नुवन् *na āpnuvan* could not reach (यस्मात् *yasmāt* since) पूर्वं अर्षत् *pūrvam arṣat* went before the mind. तत् *tat* It तिष्ठत् *tiṣṭhat* being steady धावतः *dhāvataḥ* running (i.e. changeable) अन्यान् *anyān* other objects अत्येति *atyeti* outstrips. तस्मिन् (सति) *tasmin sati* It being present मातरिश्वा *mātariśvā* the cosmic energy, i.e. the prāṇa (lit. air) अपः *apaḥ* all the activity (of the living beings) दधाति *dadhāti* sustains.

The Self is one. Unmoving,[1] It is faster than the mind. Having[2] preceded the mind, It is beyond the reach of the senses. Ever[3] steady, It outstrips all that run. By[4] Its mere presence, it enables the cosmic energy to sustain the activities of living beings. 4

[Notes—The distinction between the two types of men has already been drawn. Now, what is the nature of the Ātman by knowing which one is saved from spiritual suicide? This is discussed from here up to the eighth verse.

1. *Unmoving etc.*—The Ātman is the unchangeable and eternal Principle at the back of the changing Nature.

On whatever the mind alights, it finds the light of Ātman already there, because the Ātman is all-pervading. Hence It is swifter than the mind, the swiftest of all things known to us.

2. *Having preceded etc.*—The mind is subtler and infinitely faster than the senses; so if the Ātman is beyond the grasp of the mind, It is much more so beyond the powers of the senses. The Ātman is never an object of perception.

3. *Ever steady etc.*—As the Ātman is all-pervading, there is nothing that can go beyond it.

4. *By its mere presence etc.*—Being the Conscious Principle behind life, the Ātman is spoken of as the sustainer of all the activities of living beings. It should be noted here that It is spoken of only as awakening the cosmic energy into activity by Its mere presence. For, the Ātman really does no action; it is the cosmic energy that translates itself into all activities of life, mind itself being a manifestation of it. The cosmic energy is also known as *sūtrātman* and *prāṇa*.]

तदेजति तन्नैजति तद्दूरे तद्वन्तिके ।
तदन्तरस्य सर्वस्य तदु सर्वस्यास्य बाह्यतः ॥ ५ ॥

Tad ejati tan naijati tad dūre tadv'antike
tad antarasya sarvasya tadu sarvasy'āsya
bāhyataḥ ॥ 5 ॥

तत् *tat* that एजति *ejati* moves; तत् *tat* that न एजति *na ejati* moves not; तत् *tat* that दूरे *dūre* far; तत् *tat* that उ अन्तिके *u antike* near even; एतत् *etat* that अस्य सर्वस्य *asya sarvasya* of all this अन्त: *antaḥ* within; तत् *tat* that उ *u* again सर्वस्य अस्य *sarvasya asya* of all this बाह्यत: *bāhyataḥ* outside.

It[1] moves, and It moves not. It[2] is far, and It is near. It[3] is within all this, and it is also outside all this. 5

[Notes — 1. *It moves etc.*—In its real absolute state It moves not, *i.e.*, is immutable; but in Its conditioned aspect It appears to be ever-changing, ever in motion.

2. *It is far etc.—i.e.*, It is omnipresent. Or it can be explained thus: For the ignorant, It is far, *i.e.* very difficult to attain, but to the wise, It is very near, because they know It as their very Self.

3. *It is within etc,*—It is immanent and also transcendent, *i.e.* beyond creation, beyond limitation. It has two aspects, the conditioned and the unconditioned. Hence the opposite epithets are given to It.]

यस्तु सर्वाणि भूतान्यात्मन्येवानुपश्यति ।
सर्वभूतेषु चात्मानं ततो न विजुगुप्सते ॥ ६ ॥

Yas tu sarvāṇi bhūtāni ātmany'evā'nupaśyati 1
sarva bhūteṣu c'ātmānaṁ tato na vijugupsate ‖ 6 ‖

य: *yaḥ* (The wise one) who तु, *tu* and सर्वाणि *sārvāṇi* all भूतानि *bhūtāni* beings आत्मनि *ātmani* in

Ātman एव *eva* itself अनुपश्यति *anupaśyati* sees, च *ca* and सर्वभूतेषु *sarvabhūteṣu* in every being आत्मानं *ātmānam* the Atman, ततः *tataḥ* from that न *na* not विजुगुप्सते *vijugupsate* hates (rejects).

The wise man who perceives[1] all beings as not distinct from his own Self at all, and his own Self as the Self of every being—he does not, by virtue of that perception, hate[2] any one. 6

[NOTES—1. *Perceives all beings etc.*—The idea is that when the unconditioned state of consciousness is realised the wise man recognises that the one Conscious Principle (Self or Ātman), which witnesses the modifications of the body-mind combination, that is specially called his own, is the same as the Conscious Principle witnessing all other entities from the highest to the lowest.

2. *Hate anyone*—Hatred is born of self-interest, which in turn has its basis in the sense of separateness. When the unity of the Self in all is realised, there is no room for hatred.]

यस्मिन् सर्वाणि भूतान्यात्मैवाभूद् विजानतः ।
तत्र को मोहः कः शोक एकत्वमनुपश्यतः ॥ ७ ॥

Yasmin sarvāṇi bhūtāni ātma'ivābhūd vijānataḥ ।
tatra ko mohaḥ kaḥ śoka ekatvam anupaśyataḥ ॥7॥

यस्मिन् *yasmin* when विजानतः *vijānataḥ* to the knower आत्मा *ātmā* Ātman एव *eva* verily सर्वाणि *sar-*

vāṇi all भूतानि *bhūtāni* beings अभूत् *abhūt* has become, तत्र *tatra* then एकत्वं *ekatvam* oneness अनुपश्यत: *anupaś-yataḥ* of one who beholds क: *kaḥ* what मोह: *mohaḥ* delusion, क: *kaḥ* what शोक: *śokaḥ* sorrow?

What delusion, what sorrow is there for the wise man who sees the unity of existence and perceives all beings as his own Self? 7

स पर्यगाच्छुक्रमकायमव्रण-
मस्नाविरꣳ शुद्धमपापविद्धम् ।
कविर्मनीषी परिभूः स्वयम्भू-
र्याथातथ्यतोऽर्थान् व्यदधाच्छाश्वतीभ्यः समाभ्यः ॥

Sa paryagāt śukram akāyam avraṇam
asnā-viraṁ śuddham apāpa-viddham l
kavir manīṣi paribhūḥ svayambhūr-
yāthā-tathyato 'rthān vyadadhāt śāśvatībhyaḥ samābhyaḥ ॥ 8 ॥

स: *saḥ* He (the Ātman) स्वयम्भू: *svayambhūḥ* self-existent; पर्यगात् *paryagāt* (is) all-pervading, अकायं *akāyam* without body, अस्नाविरम् *asnāviram* without muscles, अपापविद्धम् *apāpaviddham* untainted by sin or ignorance; शुक्रम् *śukram* radiant, अव्रणं *avraṇam* scatheless (whole), शुद्धम् *śuddham* pure; कवि: *kaviḥ* all-seeing, मनीषी *manīṣī* all-knowing, परिभू: *paribhūḥ* encompassing all. (स: *saḥ* He) याथातथ्यत: *yāthātath-yataḥ* in the proper way शाश्वतीभ्य: *śāśvatībhyaḥ* for eternal समाभ्यः *samābhyaḥ* Prajāpatis (or years) अर्थान् *arthān* duties व्यदधात् *vyadadhāt* assigned.

He, the self-existent, is everywhere, without a body, without muscles, and without the taint of sin; radiant, whole, and pure, seeing all, knowing all, and encompassing all, He duly[1] assigned their respective duties to the eternal Prajāpatis. 8

[NOTES—1. *Duly assigned etc.*—This passage has also been explained as, "He has distributed all objects of the universe rightly for all eternity," or as "In the eternal procession, He has assigned to every period its proper duty."]

अन्धं तमः प्रविशन्ति येऽविद्यामुपासते ।
ततो भूय इव ते तमो य उ विद्यायाँ रताः ॥ ९ ॥

Andhaṁ tamaḥ praviśanti ye'vidyām upasate ।
tato bhūya iva te tamo ya u vidyāyāṁ ratāḥ ॥ 9 ॥

ये *ye* Those who अविद्यां *avidyām* avidyā उपासते *upāsate* worship, ते *te* they अन्धं *andham* blinding तमः *tamaḥ* darkness प्रविशन्ति *praviśanti* plunge ये *ye* those who उ *u* but विद्यायां *vidyāyām* in Vidyā रताः *ratāḥ* delight ते *te* they ततः *tataḥ* than that भूयः *bhūyaḥ* greater तमः *tamaḥ* darkness इव *iva* as it were प्रविशन्ति *praviśanti* fall into.

Those who are devoted[1] to avidyā (ignorance or pure ritual) enter into blinding darkness. Into darkness greater than that, as it were, do those enter, who delight[2] in vidyā (knowledge of ritualistic philosophy) alone. 9

[NOTES—The description of the nature of the Ātman that is attained by true Sannyāsins who seek knowledge alone, ends with verse 7. From here onwards the Upaniṣad addresses itself to those who wish to live here continually, doing good works, ritualistic and otherwise.

1. *Devoted to avidyā*—Avidyā literally means ignorance; but here it denotes ritualistic observances, as all rituals are performed through the ignorance of the real nature of Ātman that is beyond all action.

2. *Delight in vidyā*—Vidyā means knowledge, but here it signifies the ordinary theoretical knowledge of gods and rituals.

The drift of this verse is that those persons who remain satisfied with the performance of the rituals only, and never strive to know the real significance of the works as explained in the scriptures, are *rājasic* and cannot attain to that *sāttvic* state of life which rests upon the glorious union of the ritualistic actions with the knowledge of their full significance. But still worse are those persons who remain contented with the mere theoretical knowledge about the gods and sacrifices gathered from scriptural study, and never stir themselves up for any action. They are *tāmasic*, and as such, are necessarily relegated by their own inactivity to the inert state, which, of all levels of existence, is the one farthest away from the Truth.

It may be noted that in this interpretation, which follows Saṅkara's, the significance of the expression 'iva' or 'as it were', is not brought out. In the alternative interpretation of the Upaniṣad given at the end of the book, we have tried to make some meaning out of it.

Some commentators hold that here vidyā means the theoretical knowledge of Brahman gained from mere study.]

अन्यदेवाहुर् विद्यया अन्यदाहुरविद्यया ।
इति शुश्रुम धीराणां ये नस्तद्विचचक्षिरे ॥ १० ॥

Anyad ev'āhur vidyayā anyad āhur avidyayā
iti śuśruma dhīrāṇāṁ ye nas tad vicacakṣire
॥ 10 ॥

विद्यया *vidyayā* By vidyā, अन्यत् *anyat* a different (फलं *phalam* result) आहुः *āhuḥ* they say, अविद्यया *avidyayā* through avidyā अन्यत् *anyat* a different एव *eva* verily आहुः *ahuḥ* they say; इति *iti* thus धीराणां *dhīrāṇām* from the wise शुश्रुम *śuśruma* we have heard, ये *ye* who नः *naḥ* to us तत् *tat* that विचचक्षिरे *vicacakṣire* explained.

One result, they say, is obtained[1] by vidyā (knowledge of ritualistic philosophy), and quite another by[2] avidyā (ignorance or pure rituals). Thus have we heard from the wise who explained it to us. 10

[NOTES 1. *Obtained by vidyā*—The goal obtained by ritualistic knowledge is the world of the gods.

2. *By avidyā*—The goal of pure rituals is the world of the manes.]

विद्यां चाविद्यां च यस्तद्वेदोभयं॑ सह ।
अविद्यया मृत्युं तीर्त्वा विद्ययाऽमृतमश्नुते ॥ ११ ॥

Vidyāṁ c'āvidyāṁ ca yas tad ved'obhayaṁ saha
avidyayā mṛtyum tīrtvā vidyayā'mṛtam aśnute
॥ 11 ॥

यः *yaḥ* who विद्यां च अविद्यां च *vidyām ca avidyām ca* vidyā and avidyā तत् *tat* that उभयं *ubhayam* both सह *saha* together वेद *veda* knows, अविद्यया *avidyayā* by avidyā मृत्युम् *mṛtyum* death तीर्त्वा *tīrtvā* having conquered; विद्यया *vidyayā* by vidyā अमृतं *amṛtam* the nature of immortals (lit-immortality) अश्नुते *aśnute* attains.

He who understands vidyā and avidyā, both together, attains[1] to the nature of immortals through vidyā (knowledge of ritualistic philosophy), having conquered death by avidyā (pure rituals). 11

[Notes—1. *Attains to the nature of immortals etc.*—According to Saṅkara the immortality referred to here is not the absolute immortality of Brahman but the relative immortal nature of the gods. Death here means, according to him, the works and knowledge of the ordinary ignorant life, which are all subject to destruction. His object in interpreting it in this way, which looks far-fetched, is to avoid the combination of works and knowledge as a direct means of attaining supreme illumination; for these, according to him, are opposed like light and darkness, in their application to Brahman.

An alternative interpretation of this may be given if we do not go all the way with Śaṅkara in maintaining the opposition between action and knowledge. Action, ritualistic or otherwise, when done with desire, is surely opposed to spiritual enlightenment: but why should works of a purely devotional nature like communion and the rest, which help us to reduce the theoretical knowledge of Brahman into an actual realisation in life, be also regarded as opposed to enlightenment? If, therefore, we take vidya and avidyā to mean theoretical knowledge of Brahman and the devotional practices necessary for its actual realisation respectively, then the passage may be given a more direct interpretation. By avidyā or devotional practices, including selfless work, we overcome '*mṛtyu*' or the ordinary life of birth and death, and by vidyā or Knowledge of Brahman we attain absolute immortality. What is meant is that mere conceptional knowledge of Brahman is not enough; it must be combined with the practice of spiritual disciplines. The mere theorisation of Brahman is not the realisation of Brahman; for without combining practice with it, the theory will not be able to counteract the mental and physical tendencies that obstruct the dawning of Knowledge.]

अन्धं तमः प्रविशन्ति येऽसम्भूतिमुपासते
ततो भूय इव ते तमो य उ सम्भूत्यां रताः ॥ १२ ॥

Andhaṁ tamaḥ praviśanti ye'sambhūtim
upāsate ।
tato bhūya iva te tamo ya u sambhūtyāṁ ratāḥ
॥ 12 ॥

ये *ye* who असम्भूतिम् *asambhūtim* non-becoming उपासते *upāsate* worship ते *te* they अन्धम् *andham* blinding तमः *tamaḥ* darkness प्रविशन्ति *praviśanti* enter; ये *ye* who उ *u* but सम्भूत्या *sambhūtyā* in becoming रताः *ratāḥ* delight ते *te* they ततः *tataḥ* than that भूयः *bhūyaḥ* much greater इव *iva* as it were तमः *tamaḥ* darkness (प्रविशन्ति *praviśanti* enter).

Those who worship *asambhūti*[1] (non-becoming or Prakṛti) enter into blinding darkness. Into darkness still greater than that, as it were, do they enter who delight in *sambhūti*[2] (becoming or Hiraṇyagarbha). 12

[Notes—1. *Asambhūti*—i.e., Prakṛti or Māyā, the non-intelligent first Cause of the universe, in a state of equilibrium, before the creation.

2. *Sambhūti*—Signifies the Hiraṇyagarbha, the first manifestation of Brahman. He is known by different names, viz., Brahmā, Sūtrātman, Kāryabrahman, etc. Māyā playing upon Brahman causes the first manifestation of Hiraṇyagarbha in the beginning of the cycle. He, in turn, creates the whole universe.]

अन्यदेवाहुः सम्भवादन्यदाहुरसम्भवात् ।
इति शुश्रुम धीराणां ये नस्तद्विचचक्षिरे ॥ १३ ॥

Anyad ev'āhuḥ sambhavāt anyad āhur asambhavāt 1
iti śuśruma dhīrānām ye nas tad vicacakṣire ॥13॥

सम्भवात् *sambhavāt* From (the worship of) the becoming (Hiraṇyagarbha), अन्यत *anyat* different एव *eva* verily (फलं *phalam* result) आहु: *āhuḥ* they say, असम्भवात् *asambhavāt* from (the worship of) the non-becoming (Prakṛti) अन्यत् *anyat* a different (फलं *phalam* result) आहु: *āhuh* they say; इति *iti* thus धीराणाम् *dhīrāṇām* from the wise शुश्रुम *śuśruma* we heard, ये *ye* who न: *naḥ* to us तत् *tat* that विचचक्षिरे *vicacaksire* explained.

One[1] result, they say, is obtained from the worship of *sambhava* (the becoming or Hiraṇyagarbha), and a quite another from that of *asambhava* (the non-becoming or Prakṛti). Thus have we heard it from the wise who explained it to us. 13

[NOTES—1. *One result etc.*—Śaṅkara says that the result of worshipping sambhūti or sambhava (Hiraṇyagarbha) is the attainment of eightfold yogic powers; and of worshipping asambhūti or asambhava (Prakṛti), absorption in Prakṛti.]

सम्भूतिं च विनाशं च यस्तद्वेदोभयं᳭ सह ।
विनाशेन मृत्युं तीर्त्वा सम्भूत्याऽमृतमश्नुते ॥ १४ ॥

Sambhūtiṁ ca vināśaṁ ca yas ted ved'obhayaṁ saha
vināśena mṛtyuṁ tīrtvā sambhūtyā'mṛtam aśnute ॥ 14 ॥

(अ *a*) सम्भूतिम् *sambhūtim* Non-becoming (prakṛti) च *ca* and विनाशम् *vināśam* destruction (i.e. the becoming or Hiraṇyagarbha) च *ca* also यः *yaḥ* who तत् *tat* those उभयम् *ubhayam* both सह *saha* together वेद *veda* knows; विनाशेन *vināśena* by (the worship of) Hiranyagarbha मृत्युम् *mṛtyum* death तीर्त्वा *tīrtvā* overcoming असम्भूत्या *asambhūtyā* through (the devotion to) Prakṛti अमृतम् *amṛtam* deathlessness अश्नुते *aśnute* attains.

He who understands *asambhūti*[1] and *vināśa*[2] both together, attains immortality[3] by devotion to *asambhūti* (the non-becoming or Prakṛti), having conquered death[4] by the worship of *vināśā* (the destruction or Hiraṇyagarbha). 14

Notes—1. *Asambhūti*—In the text there is the word *sambhūti* in the 1st line and *asambhūti* in the 2nd. But Śaṅkara says that *sambhūti* in the 1st line should be taken as an aphaeresis of *asambhūti*, the initial 'a' being elided; and in the 2nd line he reads, '*Vināśena mṛtyuṁ tīrtvā sambhūtyā*,' where '*tīrtva*' and '*asambhūtyā*' are combined euphonically. Therefore he holds that *sambhūti*, *i.e.*, *asambhūti*, means the non-becoming or the unmanifested Prakṛti referred to in the previous verses.

2. *Vināśa*—This word means 'destruction', but here it should be taken as 'destructible', *i.e.*, abstract used

for the concrete. Whatever is caused, is destructible. So Hiraṇyagarbha, being the first manifestation of Brahman, is also destructible. Hence by the word vināśa, as by *sambhūti*, (becoming) in the preceding verses, Hiraṇyagarbha is meant. Through the worship of Hiraṇyagarbha, one can get great occult powers.

3. *Immortality*—Here it means absorption in Prakṛti. By intense concentration on Prakṛti, one remains absorbed in it till the end of a cycle, and at the beginning of the next cycle is born as the presiding deity of a certain sphere of existence.

4. *Death*—Limited powers of worldly life. The worship of Hiraṇyagarbha gives supernatural powers.

It is very difficult to make out the real meaning of verses 12, 13 and 14. What is given here is the view of of Śaṅkara, the drift of which is that the combined worship of Prakṛti and Hiraṇyagarbha takes one to the highest position attainable through work. The opposition between work and Knowledge is here taken for granted.

Among the other commentators, Uvaṭācārya gives a more plausible meaning of the 14th verse. He takes sambhūti to mean Brahman, the cause of all creations and vināśa, the body which is perishable. He explains the whole verse thus: The Yogin who knows both Brahman and the (secret of) body attains immortality through the Knowledge of Brahman, having crossed death through works performed with the body and productive of jñāna.

Then again, if we do not accept the opposition between Knowledge and work, we may interpret the passage in the same way as we have done for the 9th, 10th and 11th verses. We can take sambhūti and asambhūti in the last three verses to mean work (karma) and Knowledge (jñāna) respectively ; and in the 14th verse sambhūti may be taken as an aphaeresis of asambhūti, meaning Knowledge, and vināśa as work, since all work is perishable.]

हिरण्मयेन पात्रेण सत्यस्यापिहितं मुखम् ।
तत् त्वं पूषन्नपावृणु सत्यधर्माय दृष्टये ॥ १५ ॥

Hiranmayena pātrena satyasy'āpihitaṁ mukhaṁ
tat tvaṁ pūṣann apāvṛṇu satya-dharmāya
dṛṣṭaye ॥15॥

हिरण्मयेन *Hiranmayena* Golden पात्रेण *pātreṇa* with the plate (orb of the sun) सत्यस्य *satyasya* of the truth मुखम् *mukham* entrance अपिहितम् *apihitam* (अस्ति *asti*) is covered. पूषन् *pūsan* O Sun (lit. the supporter) तत् *tat* that सत्य धर्माय *satyadharmāya* for me who is devoted to the true दृष्टये *dṛṣṭaye* to the view त्वम् अपावृणु *tvam apāvṛṇu* do thou remove.

Like a lid, Thy shining golden orb covers the entrance[1] to the Truth in Thee. Remove it, O Sun, so that I who am devoted to the True may behold That. 15

[NOTES—According to Śaṅkara the Upaniṣad explains, from here onwards, by what path those who have been devoted all their life to scripture-enjoined works and the worship of lower Brahman, attain immortality after death. This and the succeeding verses form the prayer of such a devotee.

1. *Entrance to the Truth*—In the Upaniṣads (Vide Chāndogya, III. 19, 4, VIII, 3. 3, IV. 15. 1 ; Bṛhad., II. 1. 2, IV. 3. 6, II. 3. 5 ; Kauṣītakī, IV. 3; Kaṭha, VI. 9) one is advised to meditate upon Brahman as residing in the sun, the heart, and the eyes, because special manifestations of Divine glory are associated with these regions. This particular verse is the dying prayer for the illumination of one who has been devoted all through his life to the contemplation of the Deity as manifested in the sun. He wants to see the spiritual entity behind the shining orb of the material sun.]

पूषन्नेकर्षे यम सूर्य प्राजापत्य
व्यूह रश्मीन् समूह ।
तेजो यत् ते रूपं कल्याणतमं
तत् ते पश्यामि योऽसावसौ पुरुषः सोऽहमस्मि ॥१६॥

pūṣann ekarṣe yama sūrya prājāpatya
vyūha raśmīn samūha ।
tejo yat te rūpaṁ kalyāṇa-tamaṁ
tat te paśyāmi yo' sāv'asau puruṣaḥ
so'ham asmi ॥ 16 ॥

पूषन् *pūṣan* the supporter एकर्षे *ekarṣe* the lonely courser यम *yama* the controller प्राजापत्य *prājāpatya* the son of Prajāpati सूर्य *sūrya* O Sun रश्मीन् *raśmīn* the rays व्यूह *vyūha* remove, तेजः *tejaḥ* light *samū-*

ha withdraw. यत् *yat* which ते *te* thy कल्याणतमं *kalyāṇatamam* the most glorious, the most रूपम् *rūpam* form तत् *tat* that ते *te* (प्रसादात *prasādāt*) through Thy grace पश्यामि *paśyāmi* I behold. यः *yaḥ* Who असौ *asau* that पुरुषः *puruṣaḥ* Being सः *saḥ* He अहम् *aham* I अस्मि *asmi* am.

O Sun, offspring of Prajāpati, Thou lonely courser of the heaven, Thou controller and supporter of all, contract Thy rays, withdraw Thy light. Through Thy grace, I behold the most blessed form of Thine. I am indeed He, that Being who dwells there. 16

वायुरनिलममृतमथेदं भस्मान्तं शरीरम् ।
ॐ क्रतो स्मर कृतं स्मर क्रतो स्मर कृतं स्मर ॥ १७ ॥

Vāyur anilam amṛtam ath'edaṃ bhasm'āntaṁ
śarīram ।
Om krato smara kṛtaṁ smara krato smara kṛtaṁ
smara ॥ 17 ॥

अथ *atha* Now वायुः *vāyuḥ* the breath अमृतम् *amṛtam* the eternal अनिलम् *anilam* the (all-pervading) air (प्रतिपद्यताम् *pratipadyatām* let attain). इदम् *idam* this शरीरम् *śarīram* body भस्मान्तम् *bhasmāntam* reduced to ashes (भूयात् *bhūyāt* let be) ओं *Om* om. क्रतो *krato* O mind कृतम् *kṛtam* deeds स्मर *smara* remember.

Now let my breath be merged in the all-pervading immortal Prāṇa, and the body be reduced to ashes. Om. Mind! remember[1], past deeds remember! Mind! remember, past deeds remember! 17

[NOTES—This and the next verse form the prayer of the devotee of pious works at the time of death.

1. *Remember etc.*—The probable significance of the passage is this: As the course of the departing soul entirely depends upon the predominant thoughts at the dying moment, the devotee is, at the time of death, asking the mind to fill itself with the memories of all the good deeds of his life, so that he may take the higher passage referred to in the next verse. Cf. Bhagavad-gīta, VIII.6.]

अग्ने नय सुपथा राये अस्मान्
विश्वानि देव वयुनानि विद्वान्।
युयोध्यस्मज्जुहुराणमेनो
भूयिष्ठां ते नमउक्तिं विधेम ॥ १८ ॥

Agne naya supathā rāye asmān
viśvāni deva vayunāni vidvān
yuyodhy'asmaj juhurāṇam eno
bhūyiṣṭhāṁ te nama uktiṁ vidhema ॥ 18 ॥

अग्ने *agne* O Agni अस्मान् *asmān* us राये *rāye* to the enjoyment of the fruits of our karma सुपथा *supathā* by the fair path नय *naya* take, lead. देव *deva*

O Lord, विश्वानि *viśvāni* all वयुनानि *vayunāni* deeds विद्वान् *vidvān* knowing अस्मत् *asmat* from us जुहुराणम् *juhurāṇam* crooked going, deceitful एनः *enaḥ* sin युयोधि *yuyodhi* destroy ते *te* to Thee भूयिष्ठाम् *bhūyiṣṭhām* very many नम उक्तिम् *nama uktim* words of salutations विधेम *vidhema* do we offer.

O Agni, lead us by the fair[1] path that we may reap the good we have sown. Thou knowest all our deeds. Lord, destroy all crooked-going sins in us. We salute Thee with[2] our words again and again. 18

[NOTES—1. *Fair path*—Reference is made here to the deva-yāna or 'the path of the gods'. In the Vedānta two paths are mentioned, by which the departed souls may proceed to enjoy the fruits of karma done during their life on the earth. One is called deva-yāna, 'the path of the gods" or arcirmārga, 'the path of light" and the other pitṛ-yāna, 'the path of the manes', or dhūmamārga 'the path of darkness'. The former leads to the region of Brahmā, known as satya-loka, through the different spheres, such as the planes of Agni, the day, the bright half of the lunar months, *i. e.*, 'śuklapakṣa' the six months of the sun's passage to the northern solstice, the year, the devas, the vāyu, the sun, the moon, the lighting, the region of Varuṇa, the region of Indra, and the region of Prajāpati. The pitṛyāna, on the other hand, leads to candra-loka or the region of the moon, through quite a different path consisting of spheres such as those of smoke or darkness, night, the six months of the sun's passage to the southern solstice, year, the pitṛloka, *i.e.*, 'the world of the manes', and the ether. One who goes by the devayāna, has not to come back again to this world, but remains in the Brahma-loka till the end of the cycle, when he attains complete absorption in Brahman with Brahmā. This process of emancipation is called kramamukti or gradual or indirect salvation in contradistinction of Jivan-mukti or direct salvation even while alive in the body, which is attained only by the realisation of the true nature of the Self. None but those who worship the Saguṇa-brahman (Brahman in Its qualified aspect), the Naiṣṭhika-brahmacārin, *i.e.*, one who observes lifelong vow of sexual purity, the Vānaprasthin, *i.e.*, one who leads the retired life of worship and devotion in the forest, and the Gṛhastha or house-holder knowing the pañcāgni-vidyā (Chāndogya, V. 3 .1), are eligible for the deva-yāna. But all others who are of ordinary knowledge and actions, and do some charitable or good works in their lifetime, go, when they depart, to Candra-loka by the other path ; and there they remain for the enjoyment of the fruits of their good karma till its exhaustion. Then they come back again with some residue of their past karma, to be reborn on this earth to undergo all the pains and pleasures of life here. Cf. Bhagavad-gītā, VIII, 24 & 25.

So in the 18th verse, the devotee is ardently praying to Agni to take him by deva-yāna that he may not have to come back again into this world of misery. Since Agni was considered the principal intermediary god for an Agnihotrin (one who worships Agni)—for through Agni he offers all his oblations to other gods even—the devotee is praying to Agni with the assertion, "Thou knowest all our deeds, O Lord."

2. *With our words*—The devotee wants to say that he is dying, and therefore he has no strength left to do the whole worship. So he is offering salutations by word of mouth only.]

ॐ पूर्णमदः पूर्णमिदं पूर्णात् पूर्णमुदच्यते ।
पूर्णस्य पूर्णमादाय पूर्णमेवावशिष्यते ॥

ओं शान्तिः । शान्तिः । शान्तिः ॥

Om Peace ! Peace ! Peace.

APPENDIX

The study of the ancient religious literature of India reveals that from the Vedic time onwards there were two main currents of philosophic thought in this country. One insisted on the importance of rituals (karma) and the attainment of heavenly felicity through them, while the other minimised the value of these and emphasised the intution of Brahman through Knowledge and ascetic practices as the goal of human life. The difference in these two philosophies affected the whole scheme of life advocated by the two groups expounding them, the first preferring an active life in society and the second a life of retirement and mystic absorption. The karma-kāṇḍā of the Vedas, comprising the Samhitas and the Brāhmaṇas, was the source of inspiration for the former, while the latter based their philosophy of life on the jñāna-kāṇḍa of the Vedas consisting of the Āraṇyaka and the Upaniṣads. It was, however, only in later times when these two typical doctrines in Vedic thought came to be systematised by Jaimini and Vyasa, that the distinction between them became well-defined. Henceforth they received the distinct names Mīmāṁsā and Vedānta, the Advaitins among the Vedāntins holding that the latter system is no way directly related to the former.

But it cannot be denied that even in the Vedic days the difference between these two schools of thought was felt in a sufficiently acute form. Consequently, as in later times, some of the best thinkers of the day must have felt the necessity for effecting a reconciliation between them. And most probably the Īśāvāsyopaniṣad is one such striking attempt. According to literary history the Śukla-yajurveda or the Vājasaneyi-saṁhitā, of which the present Upaniṣad is the 40th chapter, was comparatively of much later origin than the rest of the Vedic literature, and it seems all the more likely that the thinkers of this period should have felt all the more the need of reconciling the two streams of thought. Īśāvāsyopaniṣad, according to some, is an early effort in this direction.

In the translation and the notes given in the body of the book, we have followed Śaṅkara's interpretation of the Upaniṣad. Śaṅkara was one of the most prominent Vedāntic thinkers of post-Vedic times, holding strong views about the relation between karma and jñāna. According to him, ritualistic work and Brahman-intuition are contradictory like light and darkness; for karma is based upon the ego-sense and desires, and jñāna on their destruction. They cannot therefore be simultaneously combined. They can be reconciled only by allotting them to different stages of spiritual life. Karma of all kinds, he relegates to the pre-Knowledge stage. When performed with desire, karmas, whether ritualistic or altruistic, bestow on one merits that entitle one to certain transient enjoyments in this world and in heavenly regions. When performed without coveting the fruits for oneself and as an offering unto the Lord, the same karmas lead to the purification of the mind, which is the stage preparatory to spiritual enlightenment or Knowledge. After the mind is purified, the aspirant has no concern with work of this kind even. He has only to listen to the Upaniṣadic teachings and absorb himself in medition on them—a task for which he has attained the necessary capacity by means of the purification of the mind achieved through disinterested karma. One who has not yet attained this state of mental purity must go on doing distinterested karma in a spirit of dedication to the Lord. He too will attain Knowledge gradually, but not immediately here on earth. By virtue of his actions and devotions he will go to the highest heaven, live there till the end of the cycle, and then attain Knowledge and complete emancipation. The way of attainment is called krama-mukti or gradual emancipation, as distinguished from the other kind known as Jīvanmukti or liberation in this very embodied state. Thus according to Śaṅkara karma can only precede jñāna, not co-exist with it. And in saying this, it is also fair to state that he excludes from the category of karma vidvat-karma or actions performed by the 'knowing ones' for the good of the world without any egoistic promptings.

It is from this point of view that Śaṅkara interprets this difficult Upaniṣad and no one can deny that he makes a very consistent meaning out of it. There are, however, thinkers who do not see eye to eye with him in regard to the way in which he effects the reconciliation. They maintain that even though Śaṅkara's theory is as perfect as a theory could possibly be, it is not without a loophole. If the study of the Upaniṣads and meditating on their meaning are not considered work, and therefore regarded as reconcilable with Knowledge, why not the same be done also with disinterested action performed in a spirit of devotion? The reply of a Śaṅkarite would be that the study of the Upaniṣads and meditation, though apparently forms of work, should not be called work, because they lead directly to the destruction of the ego which is the basis of karma. The others can very well retort that the same is the case with devotion and disinterested actions too. They also rule out the ego, and are therefore no more opposed to Knowledge, or a merely indirect means to it, than the study of the Upaniṣad and meditation on them. Hence to them Knowledge and work of the higher type are not contradictory, and can and ought to be practised simultaneously for the growth of a healthy spiritual life. According to the view of these thinkers, this Upaniṣad, like the Gītā in later times, is a plea for combining Knowledge with distinterested action, perception of the many with absorption in the One, and devotion to the Personal Deity with the intuition of the Absolute. The Īśāvāsyopaniṣad can very well be construed in this light too, but, in doing so, one has to give arbitrary meanings to certain expressions: the liberty taken in this respect is not in any way greater than what has to be taken for construing it as Saṅkara has done. The difficulty is largely due to the play upon words in the text. We therefore give below a free paraphrase of the Upaniṣad in this light, changing the translation only where the new approach to the subject requires it:

WORK AND KNOWLEDGE RECONCILED

1. Whatever there is changeful in this ephemeral world — all that should be covered by the Lord. Therefore enjoy the world after renouncing desire for these ephemeral things. Do not crave for possessions.

2. Only performing work in the world, should a man desire to live the full span of his life. If he lives as mentioned before, renouncing desires and seeing the Lord in everything, he will not be subject to the natural consequences of works, namely, their good and bad fruits and rebirths resulting from them; for then works will not taint him as he is detached.

THE STATE OF THE UNSPIRITUAL

3. Those who do not recognise the Self in everything practically commit suicide. They are enshrouded in the blinding darkness of ignorance and are reborn in various spheres clouded in darkness.

NATURE OF ATMAN AND THE STATE OF SELF-REALISATION

4. The Self is one. Unmoving, It is faster than mind. Having preceded the mind, It is beyond the reach of the senses. Ever steady, It outstrips all that run. By Its mere presence, It enables the cosmic energy to sustain the activites of living beings.

5. It moves, and It moves not. It is far, and It is near. It is within all this and It is also outside all this.

6. The wise man who perceives all beings as not distinct from his own Self at all, and his own Self as the Self of every being—he does not, by virtue of that perception, hate anyone.

7. What delusion, what sorrow is there for the wise man who sees the unity of existence and perceives all beings as his own Self?

8. He, the self-existent, is everywhere—without a body, without muscles, and without the taint of sin; radiant, whole, and pure; seeing all, knowing all and encompassing all. He duly assigns their respecetive duties to the eternal Prajāpatis.

RECONCILIATION OF CONTRADICTIONS; ONE AND THE MANY, THE ABSOLUTE AND THE PERSONAL

9. Those who are engrossed in 'ignorance' or the perception of the many enter into blinding darkness. Into darkness that *seems* to be even greater than that, enter they who are absorbed in Knowledge or mystic conscious-

ness of the One in trance; for the former this is access to life and its possibilities while in the latter even this is *apparently* denied[1]

10. Thus one result, they say, is obtained by engrossment with the many (avidyā), and quite another by absorption in the One. Thus have we heard from the wise who explained it to us.

11. But he who understands the secret[2] of the many and has also absorption in the One simultaneously, attains the spiritual felicity of transcendence by absorption in the One (vidyā), having overcome the weakness[3] and delusions of mortal life by knowing how the many are the becomings of the One (avidyā).

---

1. In this and in the 14th verse absorption in the One and the Absolute is not really condemned. It only states the apparent or popular view. That is the force of 'iva', as it were, in the text.

2. Engrossment with the many without knowing the One behind it is the bane of 'ignorant' life. The secret of the many is that the One can appear to be many without losing Its unity.

3. On knowing the One, the many lose their binding influence on the seer.

12. Those who are engrossed with the worship of the 'Born' or a Personal God[1] who is not recognised as an expression of the Absolute (asambhūti and vināśa of verse 14),—enter into blinding darkness. Into darkness that *seems* even greater than that, enter they who are absorbed in the Unborn or the Absolute (asambhūti = sambhūti of verse 14): for in the former there is expression of life, while the latter *apparently* looks like inertness and negation of life.

13. Thus one result, they say, is obtained by worship of a Personal God (sambhūti), and quite another by absorption in the Absolute (asambhūti). Thus have we heard from the wise who explained it to us.

14. But he who understands the secret of the Personal Deity (*i.e.*, knows Him to be the manifestation of the Power of the Absolute) and has absorption in the Absolute simultaneously, attains the spiritual felicity of transcendence by absorption in the Absolute, having[2]

---

1. This is the stage of polytheism and is, therefore, a very low stage. The personal God of verse 14 is Īśvāra or Power of the Absolute. The Personal Deity can be called Born, because it comes from Absolute and is absorbed in it.

2. The true devotee is unmoved by the sufferings of life.

conquered the travails of life by devotion to the Personal God.[1]

KNOWLEDGE THROUGH NON-ATTACHMENT AND DEVOTION

15. Like a lid, Thy shining golden orb covers the entrance to the Truth in Thee. Remove it, O Sun,[2] so that I who am devoted to the True may behold that.

16. O Sun, offspiring of Prajāpati, Thou lonely courser of the heaven, Thou controller and supporter of all, contract Thy rays, withdraw Thy light. Through Thy grace, I behold the most blessed form of Thine. I am indeed He, that Being who dwells over there.

17. Now let my breath be merged in the all-pervading, immortal Prāṇa, and the body be reduced to ashes. Oh Mind! remember past deeds, remember! Mind! remember past deeds, remember!

18. Oh Agni, lead us by the fair path so that we may reap the good we have sown. Thou knowest all our deeds, Lord. Destroy all crooked-going sins in us. We salute Thee with our words again and again.

OM PEACE ! OM PEACE ! OM PEACE!!!

---

1. The superiority of the ideal held out in verses 11 and 14 seems to be that it combines knowledge and devotion, mysticism and work, philosophy and action, staticity and dynamism, in a harmonious way, and hence stands for an all-sided development of man, which a mere absorption in the One or the Absolute does not help.

2. Here Sun is identified with the Personal God.